Māhealani AND THE KING of HAWAI'I

by Riánna M. Williams
illustrated by Jackie Black

Ka Mea Kakau
1121 Kaimoku Place, Honolulu, HI 96821
Printed and bound in Hong Kong

AUTHOR'S NOTE

* Hawaiian *ali'i* had many names. Some were given at birth, some were given during their lifetime, and they each had a specific meaning. Some names were public names, other names were private names. Occasionally, *ali'i* were addressed by using the first line of their name chant.

* *Inoa*, one's personal name, was one's most precious possession and once spoken took on an existence that could benefit or harm the individual. For a thorough explanation of this subject see "<u>Nānā I Ke Kumu</u>", Volume 1, by Pukui, Haertig and Lee.

* There are a few Hawaiian names and words in the stories and endnotes without diacritical marks ('*okina* or *kahakō*) which might require them. These pronunciation marks give the meaning of a word, which can change, sometimes drastically, with the location of the marks. As the use of these marks is modern, it isn't known if they are needed in some words, and in others there is a question of where the marks should be placed. They have been written without marks in order to avoid creating an incorrect meaning.

* There is no letter "s" in the Hawaiian language. Therefore, the singular and plural remain the same: one *lei*, three *lei*.

* The "Hawai'i Pono'ī" sheet music is taken from <u>King's Book of Hawaiian Melodies,</u> published by Charles E. King, Honolulu, Hawai'i, copyright 1948.

PREFACE

All historical events and settings are real.

Several people mentioned in the stories were real - their backgrounds are given at the end of the book. The following people are fictional characters:

Māhealani Kanahele .... narrator and friend of King Kalākaua

Simeona Kanahele .... her father, one of the king's royal guards

Hannah Kanahele .... her mother, a cook for ʻIolani Palace servants

Rebekah .... Māhealani's aunt

Kahana, Mataio
and Wiliama .... royal guards

ʻIokepa .... ʻIolani Palace cook

Maka .... ʻIolani Palace dishwasher

TABLE OF CONTENTS

INTRODUCTION

I knew King Kalākaua. And Queen Kapiʻolani and Princess Liliʻuokalani.

But, mostly I knew the king. We were friends, even though I was a child.

I spent a lot of time in his palace, although not always with his knowledge or permission.

I'm much older now, and the days of monarchy are gone. I often think of those times, the dinners and parties and dances in ʻIolani Palace, *lūʻau*, the king telling jokes or stories about people he met and places he had been. I realize now how privileged I was to have participated, even in a small way, in those wonderful days of monarchy, and how fortunate I was to have learned about my Hawaiian heritage.

Two of my favorite royal events from my childhood were King Kalākaua's coronation and 50th birthday. I knew each one was an important occasion, but I didn't know what to expect, so I spent a lot of time wandering in and out of ʻIolani Palace being *nīele*, nosey. Sometimes I was invited and sometimes I wasn't, but I had great fun! I suppose I was given special privileges because my father, Simeona Kanahele, was one of the king's royal guards and my mother, Hannah Kanahele, worked in the palace as a cook for the servants.

I had a difficult time finding an appropriate gift for the king for these important events. What was I, a child with no money, going to give my friend, a king, that he didn't already have? How could I find a gift that would equal *umeke* [calabash], china or silver?

KING KALĀKAUA'S CORONATION

Magnificence is the first rule of kingship.

Sir John Fortescue,
The Governance of England,
published 1471

Coronation day was February 12, 1883. I didn't know what this word meant when I first heard it. I had to look it up in the dictionary, and found it meant "the ceremony of crowning a sovereign." Then I had to look up the word sovereign and found it meant "supreme in power, rank or authority."

"Māhealani," my father said, "King Kalākaua has decided to hold a coronation for himself, even though he's already been king for nine years. When he went on his nine-month trip around the world two years ago - the first monarch in history to do such a thing - he was received courteously and respectfully, as a king should be, everywhere he went."

"Why wouldn't he be treated that way, Papa?" I asked. "He is a king!"

"Well," he replied, "he came from a small kingdom and some people think that only kings and queens from large kingdoms are important.

"That's not true; it's not the size of a kingdom or country that counts, it's how the ruler treats the people and how the people are allowed to live and work that counts. The way King Kalākaua was treated on that trip made him realize that the kingdom of Hawai'i, although small and in the middle of a huge ocean, has every right to take its place beside larger, more powerful nations and royal courts of the world. Our king is a gentleman who loves his people and has great plans for his kingdom. A coronation will also be a way of celebrating our new ʻIolani Palace, just completed a few months ago."[1]

Although the palace was new, I had been inside several times, looking around in the basement and on the first floor. It was very grand and a perfect setting for parties and balls. I heard Auntie Charlotte Iaukea and other ladies talking about their new gowns and the men's new uniforms for the coronation.

Auntie Charlotte had taken me to see the pavilion that had been built for the coronation ceremony. It was attached by a walkway to the front verandah of the palace. "Along with the ceremony there will be a grand ball and a large *lūʻau*," she explained. "I will take you to the *lūʻau* because your parents will be busy, but I cannot be with you at the coronation ceremony. As one of Queen Kapiʻolani's *leke ukali* [ladies-in-waiting], I will be helping her prepare for the *poni mōʻī* [coronation]. You will be on your own, so you must be quiet and behave; none of your *hana kolohe* [mischievous behavior]."

After three days of heavy rain, the sun came out on coronation day leaving a clear, blue sky. I was excited, but also worried. Here it was, the actual day of the coronation, and I still hadn't thought of a *hoʻokupu* [gift or

offering] I could give the king. How was I going to find one? What was I going to do?

I arrived early on the palace grounds so that I wouldn't miss anything. I was wearing my best dress, made of fine white cotton with lace at the neck. I liked the dress, which my mother made, but didn't like the long sleeves, and argued with my mother when she helped me get dressed.

"No, Mama," I whined, as she buttoned the dress, "I won't wear this. The sleeves are hot and it's hard to move my arms. And I won't wear those new shoes, either. No one will look at my feet, I want to go barefoot or wear my cloth *Pākē* [Chinese] shoes."

"Māhealani Kanahele," my mother said in a scolding voice, "you will not go to the coronation unless you are dressed properly. That means your best dress and your new shoes. This is a great day of celebration for King Kalākaua, and you must honor him by being at your best."

I did understand that, even though I didn't want to admit it. I finally gave in and grumpily wore the hot dress and the new shoes, and was secretly pleased when people told me how pretty I looked.

One of the first things to be seen when approaching the palace grounds was the *Hale Keli'iponi* [coronation pavilion]. Auntie Charlotte said the words in English meant "the chief's anointing," which had to do with the actual crowning of a monarch.

"*Aloha kakahiaka* [good morning], Kahana," I said to my father's friend, also one of the royal guards, who was standing near the pavilion. "I've been to see the pavilion, but I don't know what those painted shields all around it are for. What do they mean?"

"*Aloha*, Māhealani. *Hele mai* [come]. There is time to walk around it, and I will explain everything to you. The inside of the dome, or roof, is painted blue to look like the sky or heavens. Each of the eight roof sections contains a name of the five Kamehameha kings, along with King Lunalilo, King Kalākaua, and his sister, Princess Lili'uokalani, who is the heir apparent, the next in line to the throne."

"Yes," I said knowingly, "because King Kalākaua has no children he has chosen his sister to succeed him as the next monarch. After he dies she will become queen."

The outside roof of the pavilion was decorated with red, white and blue painted stripes, and each of the roof sections had painted wood shields attached. "Those shields, Māhealani, represent the seven countries of Russia, the Netherlands, the United States, Germany, Australia, Italy, Belgium, and our own kingdom of Hawai'i.

"Under those is another shield showing our kingdom's coat-of-arms, which you recognize. Look over the entrance to the pavilion, you'll see the words 'February 12, 1883, the day on which His Majesty King Kalākaua was crowned.' The kingdom's flag is flying from the roof, and you see that peak at the very top of the roof? That represents the tip of a Hawaiian *ihe*, or spear. This is a reminder of the old days when our warriors used spears in battles."

The pillars supporting the dome were wrapped with ferns and flowers. Chairs had been placed inside the pavilion for the royal party, along with a small table. Kahana explained, "The table is to hold the royal regalia. These are special items called emblems and insignia used in the coronation, along with the written oath of allegiance to his kingdom that the king has to sign. You'll understand more about this, Māhealani, when you actually see

it happening."

This reminded me of one day when I was in the chamberlain's office, in the palace basement. The chamberlain was very important, as he was in charge of running the palace and making sure that social functions proceeded correctly. Col. Charles Judd, the chamberlain, told me about planning the coronation. "Events like coronations or grand balls or formal dinners don't just happen, Māhealani," Colonel Judd said, "they all take a great deal of preparation, sometimes nearly an entire year. The 3,500 coronation invitations, along with printed programs for the guests, were ordered many months ago from London, England. I have had many meetings with the king and members of his staff to decide on the right decorations for both outside and inside the palace, and they must be ordered and made.

"We had to decide who would give speeches, we had to discuss the appropriate music to be included, the prayers to be given, and decide when during the ceremonies each of these things would be done. Seating arrangements have to be planned according to rules of protocol, which means seating people according to their rank or place of importance.

"And new clothes had to be ordered for the entire royal family, their ʻōhua and staff. Ah, you don't know the word ʻōhua, do you? It refers to the private attendants of a chief who are actually blood relatives and who cannot be dismissed. Staff are generally, but not always, paid and can be dismissed at any time. It's an old word not used much anymore, but I like it because it easily explains the difference between them."

"What about crowns?" I asked Colonel Judd. "Have crowns been specially ordered? Will they be covered in jewels?"

"Yes, they have been ordered and will be covered in precious jewels. The two crowns are identical, except that Queen Kapiolani's is a bit smaller. That's always the case when a queen is a queen because she is the king's wife, not a queen in her own right. King Kalākaua ordered all of the royal regalia, meaning the crowns, the scepter, the sword of state and the state ring, when he was in London last year."

I asked Colonel Judd what coat-of-arms were for and what the royal regalia looked like. He showed me a huge book with a long title in German, Abildungen Zur Chronik Sammtlicher Ritter-Orden Un Ehrenzeichen.

"In English that means Illustrated and Complete Chronicle of Knighthood and Insignia," he explained. "The book tells about shields and insignia used all over the world, and it explains everything we need to know about those items when planning special royal events.

"The scepter, usually made of gold or silver or both, represents power and justice. The sword of state, also usually of gold or silver or both, represents justice and mercy. The ring signifies dignity. In most nations these items are used only for coronation ceremonies and then put away for safekeeping, although a few countries display them or use them in other ceremonies, too."

After showing me around the pavilion Kahana was called away, so I walked around the palace grounds. A huge amphitheater, also decorated with painted wood shields, flags, and greenery had been built on the grounds surrounding three sides of the coronation pavilion. Auntie Charlotte told me it could seat four thousand guests! I couldn't even imagine four thousand people, let alone all together in one place. Later she told me there were probably another three thousand people standing around inside the grounds during the ceremony. There were seats for special guests on the palace verandah, all facing the pavilion. The front pillars of the palace were decorated with colored cloth called bunting.

I suddenly noticed activity and heard noise at the front gate. I realized it must be 10 o'clock, time for the invited guests to enter the grounds. An honor guard had formed at the Kauikeaouli gate, the formal King Street gate named after King Kamehameha III. The invited guests began to enter: first came over 1,000 *haumāna*, or students, from twenty schools, then government officials, clergy from various churches, dignitaries and diplomats. Papa told me that diplomats and representatives had come from all over the world to see King Kalākaua's coronation: from England, France, Russia, the United States, Japan and several other foreign countries. These special guests were followed by the general public.

Promptly at 11:30 the palace doors opened and the formal procession began. First came *pa'a kāhili* [*kāhili* bearers]. These feather standards were the most important symbol of Hawaiian royalty, and had been used by Hawaiian *ali'i* for over one thousand years. They were so sacred there was a special room in the palace basement for storing and caring for them. It was kept locked all the time, and only the family that took care of the *kāhili* had keys to the room - even the king didn't have a key!

There were fourteen *kāhili*, made of various colored feathers from several different kinds of birds. The *kāhili* poles were made of tortoiseshell, human bones or ancient spears. I thought of those long ago chiefs and chiefesses and earlier kings and queens who had been honored with similar *kāhili*, maybe even some of the ones being used today. The *pa'a kāhili* were followed by men representing the royal household and the legislature.[2]

Next came bearers carrying the European regalia: the crowns, the scepter, the sword of state and ring. They were followed by more of the ancient

Hawaiian regalia. Kahana returned from his errand at just the right moment to continue with his explanations. "Māhealani," he said, "today will be your first chance to see Ka ʻAhuʻula o Kamehameha, the feather cloak of Kamehameha I, also called Kamehameha the Great. I know you've heard of it, but did you know it's made of over 400,000 feathers? At least 80,000 birds were needed to make such a large cloak! The cloak is truly an amazing and precious treasure. The *lei niho palaoa* is a necklace of braided human hair with a sacred pendant, made from a whale tooth. The *pūloʻuloʻu*, the kapu stick, represents sacredness."[3]

I knew about these things because Papa had explained their importance to me when I was quite young. The teeth, or *niho*, of whales, *palaoa*, were carved into hook shapes and strung onto strands of finely braided human hair, representing birthright and power. Papa said that although whale tooth ornaments were found all over the Pacific area, only the Hawaiian people carved them into hook-shaped pendants. He said no one knew for sure anymore what the shape represented, but it was most likely the *alelo*, or tongue, representing the importance of the chief's words. He told me of an old Hawaiian saying: "*I ka ʻōlelo ke ola, i ka ʻōlelo ka make*," - "In the word there is life, in the word there is death," meaning that words have great power and should be used very carefully.

Pūloʻuloʻu were displayed before chiefs or placed outside of the chief's dwelling to tell of his presence, to warn people to stay back, not to enter without invitation. Ignoring *pūloʻulo*ʻu usually, but not always, resulted in death, depending on the chief and the circumstances. That was no longer true, of course, but it still represented sacredness.

I was attracted by a large flaming torch. "And finally comes the *lama o Iwikauikaua*, the torch of Iwikauikaua, something most people don't know much about anymore," continued Kahana. "*Lama* means torch or light. Iwikauikaua was a chief about four hundred years ago, from whom King Kalākaua is descended. The *kāhili* following the torch is named after Pili, the son of Lāʻau, who was chief of Hawaiʻi about six hundred years ago. The different royal dynasties have symbols to represent their origins. The Kalākaua dynasty chose the noonday sun. Their symbol is a flaming torch at midday, just as we see it today."

It was suddenly so quiet that I was almost frightened for a minute. Then, like everyone else, I looked toward the palace doors and saw Their Majesties, King Kalākaua and Queen Kapi'olani, enter the verandah. They were escorted by Colonel Judd, the king's chamberlain, across the connecting platform and into the coronation pavilion. King Kalākaua looked serious, wearing the white uniform of the royal guards with a white helmet topped by a plume of red, white, and blue feathers.

On his chest he wore what Kahana told me were two Hawaiian royal orders, the Star and Collar of the Order of Kamehameha I and the Star of the Order of the Crown of Hawai'i. He was also wearing the foreign orders of the Star of the Order of the Chrysanthemum of Japan and the Star of the Order of St. Michael and St. George of England. Kahana said these were gifts to King Kalākaua from those countries, signifying international friendship. Now that I knew these orders had names, I decided that next time I was in Colonel Judd's office I would look these up in the big German book to learn more about them.

Queen Kapi'olani was wearing a white satin gown with gold embroidered ferns decorating the front, from the bodice to the hem. "That's Russian ermine fur on the trim," Kahana whispered. "The queen is wearing the Order of Kalākaua, the Order of Kamehameha, and the

Order of Kapiʻolani. Her gloves and slippers are embroidered in green, and she is carrying a handpainted, lace trimmed fan."

Then came the queen's ladies-in-waiting, followed by the king's sisters.[4] Princess Likelike wore a white satin brocade gown trimmed with pearls and ostrich feathers. Princess Liliʻuokalani wore a gold brocade gown with a train, and a headdress of gold leaves and white feathers. Mr. Archibald Cleghorn, husband of Princess Likelike, and their daughter, Princess Kaʻiulani followed, with John Owen Dominis, husband of Princess Liliʻuokalani and governor of Oʻahu.

Once people were in their correct places, a choir sang. Then the Honorable John M. Kapena, minister of finance, declared the king's right to the throne of the kingdom of Hawaiʻi. Princess Poʻomaikelani, sister of Queen Kapiʻolani, displayed the Hawaiian regalia to the king. Colonel Judd asked the king to swear his allegiance to the kingdom and handed him the sword of state. Princess Kekaulike, another sister of the queen, presented King Kamehameha's feather cloak to Colonel Judd, who placed it around the king's shoulders. Colonel Judd put the state ring on the king's finger and handed him the scepter.

Then I saw Prince Kawānanakoa, who was carrying the king's crown.[5] The prince handed the crown to the president of the legislative assembly, the Hon. Godfrey Rhodes, who handed it to Colonel Judd, who passed it to the king, saying "Receive this Crown of pure gold to adorn the high station wherein thou hast been placed." King Kalākaua accepted the crown and placed it on his head.

This caused head shaking and whispering among some of the guests, which I didn't understand. "What's wrong, Kahana? Did the king make a mistake?"

"No, he didn't," Kahana replied, "but, I think the king's act of crowning himself may cause confusion when the ceremony is talked and written about. Some people are not aware of a king ever having crowned himself. It's usually done by a high-ranking member of the clergy or a high-ranking government official. In England the Archbishop of Canterbury crowns the monarch, and in France it's done by the Archbishop of Reims. Many people don't understand the meaning of *mana*, the divine power of our Hawaiian *ali'i*. They don't understand that no one else in the kingdom possesses *mana* high enough to anoint

the king, so he had to crown himself. I know there is a similar custom in Siam. Ten years ago King Chulalongkorn crowned himself because there was no one of superior rank to do so."

King Kalākaua received the other crown from Colonel Judd and placed it upon Queen Kapiʻolani's head, saying "I place this crown upon your head to share the honors of my throne." The king and queen knelt, and the Rev. Alexander Mackintosh, of St. Andrew's Cathedral, and chaplain of the palace household, recited a prayer. Their Majesties returned to their seats, guns boomed from the palace grounds and from ships in the harbor, and a choir sang a song called "Coronation Anthem."[6]

While the Royal Hawaiian Band played "The Coronation March" the king and queen returned inside the palace, where the king received homage, or respect and congratulations, from his cabinet and staff, followed by another anthem sung by the choir.

The next day I learned more about the regalia.

Auntie Charlotte described everything to me in detail. "Except for the velvet cap inside the crowns, they are made of solid gold, studded with diamonds, rubies, opals, emeralds and pearls."

"Someone said the bottom rims of the crowns are circled with gold taro leaves," I said. "Is that true?"

"Yes, that's true, and it's important to know why. Taro is one of the earliest Hawaiian symbols, representing our *ali'i* as the staff of life of our people. There is an old saying, 'People who wave their hands in the air go about with empty stomachs, people who put their hands in the ground are well fed.' Do you know the word *lauloa*? This is said to be the original taro. In poetry it is sometimes referred to as *hāloa*, or long stalk, because a god named Hāloanakalaukapalili was said to have been prematurely born in the form of this taro. From his burial place came the first taro. That's why King Kalākaua specifically ordered this symbol of the Hawaiian people to be put on the European-made crowns."

She went on to say that both crowns are topped with a Maltese cross, set with diamonds, showing that this is a Christian kingdom. The silver and gold royal scepter and sword of state are decorated with symbols representing power, justice and mercy. The ring is also made of gold, with diamonds and a large red jewel called a carnelian in the center, on which is engraved the Hawaiian coat-of- arms. This is topped with an engraved crown, and below it is an engraved ribbon stating the kingdom's motto, "*Ua mau ke ea o ka ʻāina i ka pono.*" I knew this meant "The life of the land is perpetuated in righteousness," and that it came from a speech given by King Kamehameha III, in 1843.[7] Hanging from the gold leaf-covered wood ball of the *pūloʻuloʻu* was a small solid gold coat-of-arms with enamel coloring, also engraved with the kingdom's motto.

The coronation festivities were exciting, but my not having a gift for the king never left my mind. Was I going to be his only friend not to give him a *hoʻokupu*?

"What am I going to do?" I had been asking for weeks. "The king is my friend, I want to give him something special, but I don't have money to buy anything."

"No," my parents would answer, "we don't have money to buy the king an elaborate gift. Instead we give him our work and our respect and our *aloha* every day, as should you. That is our gift."

"No, Māhealani," Auntie Charlotte would say, "it isn't necessary for you to give a fancy present. Whatever you give, whether a piece of fruit from your yard or a *lei* lovingly made by your own hands, will be fine. It's the gift that comes from your heart that counts, not what it costs. And, because the king is your friend, he will appreciate it all the more." I knew this was true, but, I still wanted to give him something special.

Two days after the coronation King Kalākaua dedicated the statue of King Kamehameha I,

in front of the *Ali'iolani Hale* [government building] across the street from the palace.[8] I attended that, too, but not the formal dinner that night at the palace, because I was too young.

I was on my way home after the statue dedication, but only got as far as the next block when I decided to wander in back of the Music Hall. I often did this when no one was around. Sometimes I would find old costumes or pieces of stage sets that had been thrown away after operas or plays, and I would take them home and use them in dress-up games.

That day I found something better than ever before. I found a small, dirty kitten that I somehow knew had lost its mother. I wrapped it in a scarf I was wearing and carefully carried it home, explaining to it as we walked that it was safe, that I would take care of it. I cleaned and fed it, and when nighttime came I lay it on an old kimono in a *lau hala* [pandanus leaf] basket next to my bed. I had a dream that night about the coronation and, when I woke the next morning to happy purrs and meows, I knew I had found my gift for the king, and just in time.

The next coronation event was a ball held in the palace throne room, where guests danced European dances called waltzes, polkas, mazurkas, lancers, and schottishces, with music played by a small group of Royal Hawaiian Band members set up on the verandah. Auntie Charlotte said the guests were dressed in their finest clothes, many ordered from London and Paris. The ladies wore glittering jewels and carried fans made of ivory and lace or feathers. She said the room was decorated with ferns, palms, roses and tropical flower garlands, which scented the room as gentle breezes came in the open windows.

A day or two later was the *ho'okupu* at the palace, when the king's subjects and friends gave him gifts out of love and respect. Papa told me that this was a revival of an ancient custom, of giving a share of the bounty of the *'āina* [land] to the chief. *Konohiki*, the caretakers of the land for the chief, would collect food from the *maka'āinana*, the people who worked the land, and give it to the chief. This was the day I had been dreading for weeks, but now everything was alright because I had a wonderful gift!

Hundreds of people presented gifts to the king, some of which were later displayed in the palace. Two huge bronze vases, from the Chinese community, were eventually placed outside on the front verandah, on each side of the front doors. Some of the silver dishes and platters and centerpieces were displayed in the state dining room.

I was afraid my gift would get lost, or even hurt, with so many people coming and going. I asked Papa to take the kitten, in its basket, to the palace and leave it with someone to give to King Kalākaua. I tied a note for the king onto the basket saying that I had attended the coronation ceremony, that I was glad he was our king and my friend, that this was my gift to him and I knew he would take good care of it. I didn't want to seem rude to the queen, so I added "P.S. I hope Queen Kapi'olani will like the kitten, too." And so arrived my gift, soon to be loved and hand-fed by the king. But, I didn't know that yet.

As the afternoon went on I began to worry. Did the king even like kittens? Would the kitten stain the palace carpets and mats or tear the silk draperies? Or chew the king's shoes? Would the king and queen want a kitten wandering around inside the palace? Would they think it was a pest, and give it away? Suddenly my gift no longer seemed right. It seemed more and more like the worst present I could have given.

"I'll get it back," I decided. "I'll go to the palace basement and find which of the servants Papa gave it to and get it back. The king will never know, and somehow I'll find something else to give him."

No one in the kitchen knew where the kitten was, so I went into the basement hall to look. I

had only gone a few feet, almost to the bottom of the staircase leading up to the first floor, when I heard tiny meows followed by booming laughter - laughter I recognized and didn't expect to hear in the basement on such a busy day. I peeked around the corner, behind the staircase, and there was King Kalākaua, one hand holding a cigar, the other hand and arm gently cradling my gift as it happily tried to lick his face.

Between the meows and laughter I heard him say, "You are such a lovable little handful I'm going to name you 'Lovey.'[9] You will live in my bungalow next door, but may come into the palace when the family is here.[10] And when I see my friend, Māhealani, I will give her a special hug for giving me such a special gift!"

I was so happy I thought my heart would burst. I had done the right thing! I wanted to say something to the king, but I thought he might be embarrassed to be seen talking to a kitten. He was a kind and generous friend, always taking time to stop and talk to me, but he was a king. I thought that even kind kings might not want to be seen carrying on a conversation with a kitten! I returned home, telling everyone about my wonderful present, as if I had planned it all along. I never did tell anyone about seeing the king and Lovey in the basement, not even the queen. I thought their first meeting should be kept private.

A few weeks later I received a thank you note from Their Majesties, on official palace stationery, thanking me and inviting me to visit Lovey. I still have the note, and whenever I take it out and read it all the memories of the coronation and the dirty, forlorn little kitten come back to me.

The palace staff soon told me how King Kalākaua would carry Lovey from the bungalow to the palace, and upstairs to the second floor when it was family mealtime. Lovey would sit on the king's lap while he fed her tidbits from his plate. They said it was hard to tell who enjoyed this the most, Lovey or King Kalākaua!

I've become sidetracked, and there's still more to tell about the coronation parties. There was a boating regatta in Honolulu Harbor, a horse race in Kapiʻolani Park, and *hula* and music presented on the palace grounds. One of the

last events was a *lū'au* for nearly five thousand guests, held one afternoon on the palace grounds.

My Auntie Rebekah, who lived with us, was very excited about the *lū'au.* "Hannah," she said to my mother, her sister, "can you even imagine the quantity of food and utensils needed to serve five thousand people? Or the flowers and plants for decorations? And how many servants will they need to cook and serve the food? *Auwē!*" All of the guests didn't come and eat at one time, though. About five hundred came at a time, throughout the afternoon. They were seated on chairs and served at tables, *haole,* or "western," style. There were also many private dinners and dances held in homes throughout the islands and on some of the ships in the harbor.

It was a thrilling and busy two weeks. The ceremonies, the entertainment, and the guests who attended from all over the world confirmed

King Kalākaua's stature in the world. It was a time for the people of the kingdom of Hawai'i to stand tall and be proud. I certainly was.

Life too soon returned to its regular routine of school, playing and helping at home, all of which suddenly seemed very boring. I continued to wander around the palace grounds and in and out of the kitchen, often playing with Lovey, who got more and more spoiled, lazy and fat. Whenever I saw King Kalākaua he would smile and talk to me, or tell me a funny story. He was still my friend, even though he was now known all over the world.

KING KALĀKAUA'S 50TH BIRTHDAY

CHAPTER I

When King Kalākaua's fiftieth birthday celebration came around on November 16, 1886, I was three years older and allowed more freedom in wandering around the city, and so could attend more events by myself. "Mama," I remember saying, "fifty seems awfully old, but the king doesn't act old. He laughs a lot, loves music and dancing, and gives so many parties and dinners. He walks around town and to Waikīkī whenever he can, always looking handsome in a linen suit with his gold pocket watch dangling from his vest, wearing his straw boater or peacock quill hat and swinging a *kou* or ebony cane. I can't believe he's so old!"

"Māhealani Kauʻi Kanahele," replied my mother sternly, "fifty is not old! And even if it were, what counts is how you feel in your heart, not what the *ʻalemanaka* [calendar] says. You know the king well enough to know he is not old. *Auwē*, what silly notions you have!"

I remember the day very clearly. I awoke early, while it was still dark and quiet. Lying under

my *kapa kuiki*, the applique quilt that Mama made for me, I could take time to think. The quilt pattern was *pikake*, my favorite, and I chose the red and white colors.

I would watch the *mo'o* [lizards] chase each other up and down my bedroom wall, making their "chiking" noises, or watch the mynahs and doves in the mango tree outside my bedroom window. I wasn't really alone, my Auntie Rebekah still lived with us and was always there while my parents were at work.

Mama was already at the palace helping to cook the servants' breakfast, as they generally arrived for work at 4 a.m. She prepared food for the *'ōhua*, because it was only the special *kāne 'ā'īpu'upu'u*, the male kitchen *'ōhua*, who were allowed to prepare and cook food for *ali'i*.

Papa, still one of the king's royal guards, was at 'Iolani Barracks, behind the palace, getting ready for his part in the day's activities. He always accompanied King Kalākaua in ceremonial processions, and was part of the honor guard during formal occasions such as the opening of the legislature. A few guards lived in the barracks full time, but most lived there part-time for a certain number of days each week, returning to their homes when off duty, like my father.

On that special morning I got up right away. I quickly washed and dressed, and decided to wear my short blue dress because it was loose. I could run easily if I needed to hide before being found somewhere I shouldn't be, which sometimes happened when I was in the palace. I stood for a minute looking out at the small garden behind our house where my mother grew *'ōhi'a lomi* [tomatoes] and *nīoi* [chili peppers]. We also had banana and mango trees. Everyone grew some kind of food in their yard - what we didn't have someone else did, so we would all *pū'ai* [share]. This is our Hawaiian way, to share and take care of each other. Auntie Rebekah was already out in the yard collecting wet, fresh blossoms from our plumeria tree to make *lei* for her friends.

Mama left breakfast for me on the kitchen table, a small piece of cooked fish, left-over *poi*, and taro bread. We bought *poi* already pounded, but dry and hard, called *pa'i'ai*. We had to add water to it to make it easier to eat. My father often fished on his days off, bringing home fresh *mūhe'e* [squid] and *'opihi* [shrimp], which we would dry and use as a snack. That morning I ate quickly, so I could leave and start the day.

We lived on Garden Lane, not far from 'Iolani Palace. Mr. Wenner, the jeweler, lived down the street. He owned the best jewelry store in Honolulu, on Fort Street, where I often saw one of the royal carriages parked in front.

It was a quiet street, but the noise and activity of the city was just a few minutes walk away. Our house was small and made of wood. My mother liked to make quilts and Auntie Rebekah liked to weave *lau hala* [pandanus leaf] into baskets, all the time "talking story," usually in Hawaiian, about the old days when they were young. The kitchen was my favorite room. The table and storage part were inside, but Papa arranged it so that the cooking part jutted outside, leaving the house clean and cool.

I was an only child, but I had lots of friends living nearby. My favorite store, the Ah Sing Market, was just a block away. I often met my friends there to buy *haupia* [arrowroot and coconut cream pudding] or *kūlolo* [baked or steamed taro and coconut cream pudding]. We would sit on the old, rickety, wood benches outside, eating, talking and playing games, such as *kinikini* [marbles].

At home in the evenings Papa often told stories about things that happened at the palace, or at official ceremonies he attended with the king. "*E haʻi moʻolelo mai iaʻu,*" I would beg. "Tell me stories." And he would tell me about receptions and balls in the throne room and the government men and business men who sometimes visited King Kalākaua in his second floor office and library. I especially liked stories about the king's trip around the world in 1881: his seeing elephants and monkeys in India, riding a donkey in Egypt to visit the pyramids, meeting Pope Leo XIII in the Vatican, or having dinner with Queen Victoria at Windsor Castle. These were such exotic stories I could never get enough of them, and happily listened to them over and over again.

Although I was in a hurry that morning, I decided to take a detour past Honolulu Harbor. Once again, I didn't have a proper gift for King Kalākaua. I still didn't have any money and didn't know what to do. Maybe I would get an idea passing through downtown and the harbor area.

My friends and I loved watching ships arrive. They were usually huge, three-masted schooners or brigantines. They had lots of masts and canvas sails and sometimes strange cargo, and were full of people pointing and shouting orders. We couldn't always understand what they were saying because the ships and people often came from foreign countries, sometimes from countries we had never heard of.

It was exciting to watch the ships being unloaded. Big wooden crates of soap and grain, hardware and books, candles and tea - just about anything you could think of - would be hauled up from the bottom of the ship and heaved over the side onto the dock. This was always accompanied by us holding our breath for fear that the ropes or nets would snap, sending a precious crate into the water.

Sometimes we went to the far, ʻEwa, side of the harbor, hoping to see cows or horses being unloaded. Hanging in canvas belly straps, one by one they would be heaved up and over the side of a ship, and then have to swim and walk their way through the watery marsh onto shore, all the time their eyes huge and bulging from fear. But, how much better than the old days, when the animals had to swim to shore with their heads tied to the sides of longboats.

There was always lots of noise and activity and confusion at the harbor, but I liked that. It kept me from being noticed, and I could wander around and watch everything and listen to people talk in languages that made no sense to me at all. They wore all kinds of clothes and carried odd shaped boxes and bags, making us imagine all kinds of strange things inside. But, that day I was just taking a quick look, and didn't stay.

I ran the few blocks to 'Iolani Palace, but slowed to a walk as I got near the palace walls. The high stone and stucco walls were nearly twice my height, and even though I couldn't see into the grounds until I arrived at a gate, I was sure I could feel the *mana* of *ali'i* as I approached the royal enclosure. This divine power or spiritual energy is to be respected and honored at all times. Some of the *makule* [old people] were frightened they would offend the *mana*. But not me; it made me feel safe and protected.

There were four gates that opened into the palace grounds, each with its own name and use. Papa had told me about them years ago. "Māhealani, it's important that you know about the gates. They mean something about our history. All four gates are named after a member of our *aliʻi*. They are all decorated with the kingdom's coat-of-arms, made out of wood and painted in white, red, blue and gold. You've seen these shields many times, but may not know their meaning.

"The center of the shield shows the symbols of the Hawaiian flag and the *pūloʻuloʻu*, the sacred kapu sticks. Above those symbols is a gold crown, and on each side is a chief holding an *ihe* and a *kāhili*. Underneath is the kingdom's motto, which means that our *ʻāina* [our land, our life] can be saved for the future only by preserving it, by taking care of it."

I always used the Hakaleleponi gate, the gate at the back. This walkway was originally called Chief's Lane, but was now named Palace Walk. The gate was named after Queen Kalama, wife of King Kamehameha III, and was used by staff, servants and guards. There was always a guard posted at each gate, day and night. No one could enter unless they knew the daily password or their name had been given to the guard by the chamberlain. Since my father was a royal guard, all the guards knew me and let me pass.

I saw that Mataio, my father's best friend, was on duty that day. He smiled and saluted me as I entered. I hurried along the hard packed sand road, between Hale 'Ākala, the royal bungalow, and the recently-planted Indian banyan tree, down a short flight of steps and into the kitchen. There was a lot of noise and activity. Some of the servants came from foreign countries and were talking in their own languages. Pans and dishes clattered, and the *'ā'īpu'upu'u* gave orders every few minutes. The dry moat that surrounds the basement, and lets in air and light, generally kept the kitchen cool, but that day it was quite warm due to the extra cooking being done for the *lū'au* that afternoon.

To enter the kitchen from the outside I had to pass through a small storage room. The kitchen isn't as large as people might think, but, it had lots of storage cabinets built all around the room. There were two long work tables in the center, and two large wood burning stoves and a deep sink on the *'Ewa* side wall.

On the Waikīkī side were two dumbwaiters, like small movable elevators in a cabinet. They have shelves inside that go up and down by pulling ropes. I remember the first time I saw them. 'Iokepa, one of the cooks, laughed and said "Eh, *hana kolohe* [a trick], no? Food go in, disappear, empty plates come back." I was very young and didn't realize he was using concealed ropes inside the cabinet to make the shelves move.

I believed him when he said it worked by a magic trick, and was disappointed when he told me the truth. The dumbwaiters were used to serve the state dining room on the first floor and the private dining area in the second floor hall. The family quarters on the second floor were private, where only family, invited guests and ʻōhua went.

In the kitchen was a large *pahu hau* [ice box], which was a wood box filled with blocks of ice. That was where meat, milk and food that spoiled quickly were kept. Mama explained that ice first came to our islands in huge blocks in the bottom of ships, surrounded by sawdust or wood shavings which acted as insulation to keep the ice frozen. Once unloaded, the blocks were cut into various sizes and sold to people and shops, carefully stored in order to last as long as possible. By this time ice was being made in Hawaiʻi, and could be bought at the Rycroft or Nuʻuanu Manufacturing companies ice factories.

In the corner were two more ice boxes where I knew ice cream was kept. Sometimes it was bought at Hart's store, but it was usually made in the palace kitchen the day it was to be eaten. It was an unusual treat that King Kalākaua served only on special occasions. I can still remember my first taste. "Hmm," I sighed as the cold, sweet, creamy spoonful slid down my throat. "So *ono*, so good! I could eat this every day." I licked my cold lips and dipped my spoon into the container for more.

"No, you don't," growled Maka, one of the dishwashers. "That's *kūkiawā* [special], only for King and guests, no for *keiki nīele.* Hard to keep, come soft and mushy." It was difficult to keep for more than a few hours, even in the ice chests, as the warm climate would make the cream quickly turn sour. It was many years before I was able to eat ice cream whenever I wanted to, and it's still my favorite dessert.

When I was noticed in the kitchen I was always asked the same question: was I there for something to eat or was I there because I was *nīele*? We would all laugh because everyone knew I was usually there for both reasons. Today was busier than usual because of the afternoon *lūʻau* for fifteen hundred guests, but the kitchen servants still had time to tease me.

Birthday celebrations started a week before the king's actual birthday. Similar to the coronation festivities, there was a boating regatta in Honolulu Harbor, horse races in Kapiʻolani Park, operas and plays performed at the Music Hall, and dinners and dances and parties held all over the islands.

Uncle Curtis Piʻehu Iaukea, Auntie Charlotte's husband, was now the king's chamberlain. He told me about the palace decorations several months earlier, when he was sketching the decorating plans at the large table in his palace office. "It will be very much like the coronation. Each pillar will be wrapped in cotton bunting, displaying the Hawaiian national colors of red, white, and blue.

"In between each arch will be huge banners. Hawaiian flags will be flying from the railings, and larger flags and banners displaying His Majesty's royal standard and our national flag will fly from the palace roof."

It was going to be a long day. Events were to start at 6 a.m. and go straight through until late in the evening. It started with the *hoʻokupu*, which I dreaded for weeks. Hundreds of people arrived dressed in their best clothes, many wearing neck and head *lei*, and nearly all carrying a gift to show their *aloha* for the king, to wish him a long and happy life. I was worried and sad, because I once again didn't

have a gift and didn't know how I was going to get one.

The day started with the arrival of marshal of the kingdom John L. Kauluko, and the police force. They marched straight to the front palace steps and were received by King Kalākaua. Mr. Kauluko gave a speech and presented the king with a small book resting on a velvet cushion. The book was a Hawaiian Postal Savings Bank Order for $570 in gold. So much money!

King Kalākaua went inside to have breakfast, and soon the Royal Hawaiian Band arrived and took its place inside the *Keliʻiponi Hale* (coronation pavilion). After the coronation the pavilion was moved to the King and Richards Streets corner of the palace grounds, where it still stands. When Captain Henry Berger, the band leader, saw me, he pressed his arms to his side, clicked his heels together and bowed stiffly and formally, but winked at me as he straightened up. He was from Germany and always called me "leibchen," the German word for "child."

One day when King Kalākaua was talking to me about music, he told me how Captain Berger had been brought to Hawaiʻi from Germany in 1872 by King Kamchameha V. He was to lead the Royal Hawaiian Band, which had formed two years earlier. "Two

years after Captain Berger arrived," said the king, "he wrote the music and I wrote the words for our new national anthem, '*Hawai'i Pono'ī*,' meaning 'Hawai'i's Own.' I wanted an anthem that would tell the people to look up to their *ali'i* as their duty. Over the years, King Lunalilo, my sister Lili'u and I have written several anthems, but this one seems to be the most popular. Maybe that's because it's really a poem. I first named it 'Hymn of Kamehameha' because I wrote it as a tribute to Kamehameha I, the founding father of our kingdom, but I changed the name so people wouldn't think it was a church hymn." I always felt special when the king told me things like this, things that my friends didn't know.

At 9 a.m. the King's Own Voluntary Military Company took its place on each side of the palace front steps. At each side, on the bottom step, one of them held a burning *lama*, or torch, an old custom of torch bearers preceding the chief. A torch representing Iwikauikaua had been used in the coronation ceremony, too, as he was the one said to have originated the custom of burning *kukui* torches by daylight on royal occasions. King Kalākaua felt very strongly about reviving the ancient customs so the people wouldn't forget their heritage.

CHAPTER V

The formal reception took place in the throne room. On the dais, or raised platform, were the two thrones. They were made of wood covered in gold leaf, upholstered with red silk fabric. Each carved chair back was topped with a gold leafed crown. "Gothic Revival" style, it was called. The thrones and most of the palace furniture were made in America, in Boston.[11]

Between the thrones was a table on which was displayed a *kekahi ʻahuʻula*, a feather cloak. I knew from seeing it at the coronation that this was the Kamehameha Cloak that once belonged to King Kamehameha I.[12] It was made of yellow *mamo* bird feathers with some yellow *ʻōʻō* feathers mixed in, plus a few red *ʻiʻiwi* feathers. The cloak was considered as precious as fine jewels, and was rarely displayed.

I wondered what it would be like to touch it, to feel the thousands of soft, smooth bird feathers. It looked like velvet, the rich dress material I liked to rub against my face. But I would never do that, out of respect for the ancient chiefs that wore it. Kahana told me that in the beginning the birds were not hurt; they were carefully caught in nets, the feathers gently plucked, and the birds let go. And, while in the old days Hawaiians made much use of nature, they also knew it must be protected for future generations. But, as time went by, people disregarded the importance of this and killed the birds. This meant that some types of birds had almost disappeared.

Behind the table stood the *pūloʻuloʻu*.[13] It was made of a wood ball covered with gold leaf, impaled on the seven foot ivory tusk of a narwhal whale and set into a *koa* stand. I knew this was a gift to King Kalākaua from his friend, Captain Tripp, an English sea captain who killed the whale in the Arctic Ocean. The king displayed the *pūloʻuloʻu* on the dais as a reminder of the chiefs and *aliʻi* that had come before him. Against the wall, behind the dais, hung a large quilt, on which was stitched the kingdom's coat-of-arms.

On each side of the dais stood tall *kāhili*, and on each wall behind them hung two Hawaiian royal orders, encased in glass covered, gold-leafed frames. Royal orders were awards given to people by a monarch for their service to the monarch or their country. On one side were the Order of Kamehameha and the Order of the Crown of Hawaiʻi, and on the other side were the Order of Kalākaua and the Order of Kapiʻolani. The throne room walls were decorated with matching frames holding foreign orders presented to King Kalākaua from other monarchs. They were jewel-encrusted medals on colored silk ribbons, which could be removed from the frames and worn by the king or queen on formal occasions.

I could never remember what countries they represented, but Kahana knew them all by heart and told me they came from Great Britain, Sweden, Belgium, Japan, Prussia, Siam, Venezuela, Italy, Spain, Denmark, Austria/Hungary and Portugal.[14]

"Some of them have wonderful names," he said, "like the Order of the Red Eagle from Prussia, and the Order of the Rising Sun from Japan. In some cases, Māhealani, King Kalākaua was one of only a handful of people in the entire world to be given the order, which shows how highly he was thought of by other monarchs."

I knew that Auntie Charlotte would be wearing her Royal Order of Kapiʻolani during some of the birthday events. She once let me hold it, explaining that all royal medals were made in Paris. This one was named after the High Chiefess Kapiʻolani Nui, who died in 1841, and who, as an early convert to Christianity, defied Pele, the fire goddess. King Kalākaua awarded the Lady Companion Cross class to Auntie Charlotte in 1883. It was awarded for services in the cause of humanity, science and art and for services rendered to the sovereign or the kingdom.

The four sections of the cross were made of silver enameled in red, with a circular white enamel center containing a delicate solid gold crest and words. The front had a tiny gold medallion showing the likeness of High Chiefess Kapiʻolani. The backside was similar to the front, except that there was no picture medallion and the gold words were different. It hung from a silver crown topped with a loop, attached to the bow of a red and yellow striped grosgrain ribbon. This was a fancy French type of stiff, silk ribbon with raised lines of ribbing, not smooth like regular silk ribbon. I thought it was beautiful.

On the Waikīkī side of the dais were chairs similar to the thrones, but smaller, for use by the royal family and members of the privy council during the reception.

At exactly 9 a.m. the royal party entered: John L. Kauluko, marshal of the kingdom; Mr. John Colburn; Mr. John Ena, carrying two small elephant tusks resting on a velvet cushion; Mr. George Beckley, bearing the two gold royal crowns; His Excellency Curtis Iaukea,

His Majesty's chamberlain; Their Majesties, and Majors A. B. Hayley and William H. Cornwell. After they took their seats more cabinet ministers entered.

Then came several education societies headed by Princess Ka'iulani, her mother Princess Likelike, sister of King Kalākaua, and Princess Po'omaikelani, sister of Queen Kapi'olani. Each society was accompanied by *pa'a kāhili*, *kāhili* bearers. The ladies were elegantly dressed, wearing formal clothes made of fine cottons and silks, *lei* and hats. Many of them carried small ivory or sandalwood fans. Each lady also carried *'umeke* [calabash] as their *ho'okupu* to their king.

They were followed by the Hui Nihoa, headed by Her Royal Highness Princess Lili'uokalani. I had heard about the expedition to Nihoa, the tiny volcanic island leeward of the island of Kaua'i. The Princess made the visit with other *ali'i wahine*, or female ali'i, and, after returning home, they formed this society. Uninhabited, the island was known for its large bird population, so perhaps this was where Queen Kapiʻolani got some of the feathers she used in doing her feather work.

Auntie Charlotte told me that the queen had made a feather bedspread and a feather table cover, both sometimes displayed in her palace bedroom. I never entered the private second floor, so I never saw them. I was told the following year, after the queen and Princess Liliʻuokalani returned from attending Queen Victoria's Golden Jubilee in London, that Queen Kapiʻolani had taken several feather gifts with her. They were greatly admired by the European women, who had never before seen anything like them.

I was always curious about the king's Japanese room, where he displayed the bronze and cloisonné vases, the lacquer boxes, the silk embroidered tapestries and other gifts he was given by Emperor Meiji when he visited Japan in 1881. But, as *nīele* as I was, even I knew better than to try and sneak upstairs.

CHAPTER VI

Their Majesties took a short break, crossing the hall to the state dining room for lunch. While waiting, I watched the next groups line up outside for their turn to enter the throne room. These were the members of the diplomatic and consular corps, the foreign government representatives, and the heads of government departments and delegates from other Hawaiian islands. Then more societies, such as the *Ho'oulu a me Ho'ōla Lāhui.* The name means "Preserve and Increase the Race," which King Kalākaua chose as his personal motto because he was concerned about the possibility of the Hawaiian race dying out. He founded this health care organization for the Hawaiian people, and asked Queen Kapi'olani to head it. Then came the Fisherman's Society, followed by three hundred *haumāna* from various schools dressed in white with red decorations, nervously but proudly offering their *ho'okupu.*

The Honolulu Fire Department was next, and the last group was the Po'olā Association. These were the stevedores, the men who loaded and unloaded the ships in the harbor, wearing their distinctive red shirts. King Kalākaua had a special fondness for these hard working men, whom he considered friends. It was *po'olā* who, a little more than four years later, were given the sad honor of pulling the king's coffin in his funeral procession.

By 2 p.m. the formal reception was over and it

was time for the *lū'au*. I was excited watching it all, but also tired and hungry. "And still no gift for the king," I reminded myself, "not even an idea."

I was too hungry to wait for the *lū'au* to begin, so, after following the last guests out the front doors of the palace, I went around to the back and down to the kitchen to find something to eat. I wasn't supposed to eat there. My mother always told me I got in everyone's way, that I had plenty of food at home and didn't need to take food from the palace kitchen. I did it anyway, when I knew she wasn't there. The other servants always gave me some kind of *'ai māmā* [snack]. I knew the king wouldn't mind. And besides, I liked listening to the gossip. How else could I learn what was going on?

Just like the coronation *lū'au*, the food was served in relays on low tables. It wasn't the kind of *lū'au* we think of today: the tables were set with crystal goblets, silver knives, forks, and spoons, and china plates along with wood *'umeke*. I watched from the walkway, trying to stay out of the way. Auntie Charlotte passed me several times, once stopping to tell me that this was the largest *lū'au* held in thirty years. "The earlier one was in 1847," she said, "hosted by King Kamehameha III. It was held at Kaniakapupu, his home in Nu'uanu Valley, and he's said to have had 10,000 guests. That's amazing in itself, but remember, all the food and supplies had to be hauled there by horses and wagons, and most of the people arrived on horseback, some of them taking several days to get there. I can't imagine such an undertaking. My helping Pi'ehu with arrangements for this birthday celebration have been enough for me!"

"Oh, look, Auntie Charlotte," I said as I tugged on her arm when she passed by me again a few minutes later. "The *hula* is going to start. I've never seen *hula* danced anywhere except at home."

"Māhealani, I know you've heard talk about when *nā mikanele* [the missionaries] came they didn't like *hula* and made it seem nasty and wrong. They had never seen anything like it and didn't understand what it was about. But, people continued to dance *hula* in private, in their homes. *Hula* is so much more than dancing. It's a language of the heart, and language is the essence of every race of people. That's why King Kalākaua is proudly presenting *hula* in public today, because it's important."

This seemed strange. What could be important about dancing?

Auntie Charlotte read my mind. "*Hula* is another way of teaching and learning the chants, *mele* [songs] and stories of our ancestors and our culture. We enjoy watching

the movements, but each movement means something. There is much poetry in *hula*, which expresses all of our senses: sight, hearing, feeling, tasting and smelling. The hand movements are definite motions that tell the story. The stories are often genealogies, the history of our ancestors. Genealogies are how we know who we are."

"I know who I am! I'm Māhealani Kauʻi Kanahele, daughter of my mother and father. What more do I need to know?"

"Māhealani, you are not just a girl with a certain name, with brown skin and brown eyes and dark hair. Like all of us, you are part of your family that came before you. This is one of the ways we define ourselves and our *ʻohana*. *Hula* takes years of serious study. It teaches discipline along with movements. The historic meanings of the movements and words and chants must be learned. The *ʻōlapa* [dancers] must be very careful to express the true meaning of what they are doing. This was one of the ways our history was taught before we had *palapala*, writing."

I didn't know about *hula*, but I did know about

'ohana. It was a word I learned as a small child, a word with an almost spiritual meaning that should be used very carefully. Auntie Rebekah explained that *'ohā* are the small taro shoots growing out of the mother taro plant, called *kalo.* They cling together, then are broken apart and replanted, like families spreading out and forming new generations.

Hā means breath. Our word *'ohana* comes from that, meaning family in the sense of acting together, of being of one breath or sharing many breaths together. It's a special word to Hawaiian people, a word not to be used lightly.

CHAPTER VII

Late in the afternoon more guests were received by King Kalākaua, including the military companies of the King's Own and the King's Guard, which included Papa. I was so proud when I saw him in his uniform, a blue tunic with a white belt and white trousers, topped by a spiked helmet. It was very Prussian, similar to the Royal Hawaiian Band uniforms. Papa told me later that by the end of the day over 900 names had been entered in the king's birthday guest book. Imagine, over 900 people passing through the palace in one day!

I spent the afternoon wandering back and forth between the *lū'au* outside and the first floor of the palace. I had not had a good chance to see the *ho'okupu* up close, and decided this was the time to do it. I was still worried about my gift, and thought I had better see what kind of gifts the king had already received. I entered the palace my usual way, through the kitchen, going up the *koa* staircase to the first floor, passing the etched glass entrance doors, making a quick turn to my right and entering the throne room through the tall *koa* double doors.

The room was a treasure chest! I had never seen so many objects together in one place before. Gifts were in piles on the floor and on tables all around the room. I stood between the doors looking at everything. The gas lights gave the reds and golds of the room a special glow that gave it a fairy tale look. Usually I would have heard the mynah birds in the trees outside,

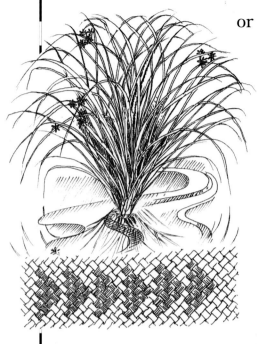

or the bells from Kawaiahaʻo Church or St. Andrew's Cathedral, or heard horse-drawn carriages passing by on King Street. But, not today, this display was too breath-taking to notice anything else.

There were more *koa* and *kou ʻumeke* than I thought anyone could possibly use, even a king. Kahana told me later that King Kalākaua received over 150 *ʻumeke* of different shapes and sizes, along with more than 100 *kāhili* of different feathers and sizes.

Mataio and Wiliama were in the room. They were both royal guards, like my father. "Eh, Māhealani, so *nīele*! You should be outside at the *lūʻau*, eating the *meaʻai ʻono* [good food]. Mataio and I have been arranging the *hoʻokupu* on the mat."

A large woven Hawaiian mat lay in front of the dais, covering most of the English wool carpet. Even as a child I was attracted to our Hawaiian mats. I often watched *kupuna*, elders, as they lovingly and carefully wove the mats. Queen Kapiʻolani was said to have a rare Niʻihau *makaloa* mat in her palace bedroom. These mats were very fine and made from the sedge plant. I knew that Princess Liliʻuokalani had a *keʻena huʻa moena*,

a room just for mats, in one of her homes. I often thought of asking her if I could see them. I knew she would have said yes, but I never asked.

'Umeke were placed in a neat triangular pattern in front of the dais, with other gifts placed on each side. There was a wood table from Queen Kap'olani, several *'umeke* from Princess Lili'uokalani, gold-decorated *kukui* nut buttons from the king's brother-in-law, Mr. Archibald Cleghorn, and a silk quilt from Mr. John Cummins. He was a high chief, who owned a sugar plantation in Waimānalo and was a close friend of the king. He was a very generous man, often giving huge *lū'au* attended by *ali'i* and commoners alike. There was sheet music of a march entitled "Makahiki Kanalima," meaning "Fiftieth Birthday," composed by Captain Berger, a gold cigar case from the employees of the General Post Office, and a silver nut bowl from the *haumāna* of the Royal School, the school the royal family had attended as children.

There was a pair of walrus ivory tusks, silver dishes and silver and china vases, paintings, and a strange-looking object that seemed to be a long, loose, soft pipe attached to a large container. "What is that thing?" I asked Wiliama. He laughed and rolled his eyes before answering. "That is a Turkish hookah, or tobacco pipe. The container holds tobacco and water. The hot smoke is drawn out through the water by sucking on the pipe.

I don't know who gave it to the king. I can't imagine him ever using it." I couldn't, either. He did smoke, but I was sure he would prefer his Cuban cigars.

Wiliama showed me a solid silver box containing fifty $20 gold coins from the officers and physicians of the Board of Health, along with a collection of letters from the men expressing their loyalty and devotion to the king. I especially liked a *kauila* wood cane topped with a solid-gold knob, inscribed with the Hawaiian coat-of-arms and the kingdom's motto, a gift from the Bureau of Customs. Around the sides of the bottom of the knob were engraved scenes of Hawai'i, with a gold band below listing the names of the donors. I knew the king would like this gift, and I could picture him walking downtown, swinging the cane and using it to point at things so that everyone could see its beauty. Mataio spent quite a bit of time holding and studying the cane. He liked to walk, and was probably dreaming about what a pleasure it would be to own such an object himself.

Although I enjoyed looking at all the gifts, I was worried about my still unknown *ho'okupu*. "Oh, Wiliama," I cried, "look at all these gifts! What am I going to give King Kalākaua? I have nothing like these carved bowls and silver boxes and paintings and gold coins!" Wiliama just shook his head, not giving me any help at all.

Mataio was gently rubbing his hands along an unusual, slender, *kou* wood container nearly three feet tall, encircled with brass bands and set in a modern *kou* stand. "This isn't a birthday gift," he said, "but the king wants to display it because of its importance. He keeps it in his bungalow next door, where he goes to relax, so few people have seen it. It's the Ipu Makani O La'amaomao, the Calabash of the Winds. It's said to be the wind container or sacred home of La'amaomao, the goddess of wind chants.

"It's supposed to have originally belonged to Lonoikamakahiki, a high chief who ruled the Ka'ū and Puna districts on our island of Hawai'i four hundred years ago. The winds could be controlled by lifting the lid and chanting to the proper wind. It was given to King Kalākaua in 1883 by Kaapana, the caretaker of the royal burial cave of Hoaiku on the sacred cliffs of Keōua, at Ka'awaloa, where the container was placed for safekeeping."[15]

"How do you know all that?" I asked, amazed at all this information.

"The story was passed on generation to generation by *kahu*, honored attendant, to *kahu*. King Kalākaua recently had a new lid made, with the calabash name engraved on a silver plate across the top, so it could be displayed today. The wide brass band around the center of the container has twelve engraved scenes copied from drawings done by James Webber, an artist who came here with Captain Cook over one hundred years ago, in 1779."

Just as when I saw the feather cloak of Kamehameha I, I felt privileged to be looking at something so ancient and sacred. Between the gifts and *lūʻau* and *hula* I was learning a great deal about my history, things that were both interesting and important to know. Auntie Charlotte's comment that I'm not just me, that I'm part of my entire family that came before me, was definitely something to think about.

CHAPTER VIII

Other gifts were displayed in the state dining room for lack of space in the throne room. There were also practical gifts such as cattle, sheep, pigs, ducks, chickens, *poi* and taro. The people who brought these live *ho'okupu* took them to the back of the palace, to a penned off area between the Indian banyan trees and the building housing the king's new electric generator. Their names and gifts would be written in the large leather bound book listing gifts and donors, to be given to King Kalākaua later. Most of the animals were given away to charitable organizations.

By this time I was tired and hungry again. I found Auntie Charlotte, told her I was going home, and that I would be back later with Mama and Auntie Rebekah to watch the parade and fireworks display, the fireworks having come from San Francisco. Papa was so busy with everything that was going on that we didn't expect to see him until the next day.

When we returned in the evening there was a slight rain, but rain has always been considered a good sign for *ali'i*, so it didn't bother anyone. Mr. John Cummins, the parade marshal, led the grand procession, starting with the Royal Hawaiian Band. They looked *nohea* [handsome] in their dark blue tunics and white caps. Several fire engine companies came next, one engine decorated with flags and banners and shooting off fireworks. The firemen also looked *nohea*, wearing red flannel shirts, black trousers and helmets, with *lei* around their necks. Each one carried a *lama*, a flaming torch. The fire company from Chinatown followed, each member swinging a colorful paper lantern. The parade ended with *haumāna* from the Royal School, also carrying *lama*.

The procession passed along Hotel Street and Maunakea Street to the corner of the palace at King and Richards Streets. It made a complete circuit around the palace, stopping before the front entrance where King Kalākaua received their shouted cheers. He seemed especially pleased with this display, expressing his *mahalo* and appreciation. The procession circled the palace two more times, gave more cheers, and then marched out the gate.

Suddenly the king's new electric lanterns lit up the outside front and sides of the Palace, followed by gasps of surprise and delight from all of us. Rockets and other fireworks were shot from the palace roof and from other areas

around Palace Square. It was a spectacular end to an exciting day, something we would never forget and would dream and talk about for years.

A grand ball was held later that evening in the throne room. I wasn't invited, of course, but I was told later and read in the newspapers that it was lovely and elegant, in the true tradition of royalty.

CHAPTER IX

Oh, yes, my gift. I haven't mentioned what I finally gave the king for his birthday. For some unknown reason, I kept looking at the set of *kukui* nut buttons from Mr. Cleghorn while I was in the throne room. Wiliama noticed my interest and said, "*Kukui* nuts used to be burned for light, and so are a symbol of enlightenment, of knowledge. And since a flaming torch at midday is the symbol of the Kalākaua dynasty, I'm sure that is why Mr. Cleghorn chose that kind of button for his *hoʻokupu*."

Then I suddenly remembered something and knew I had my gift! It had been at home in a drawer in my bedroom all this time, and I had never given it a thought. Several years before, when I was quite young, my *tūtū wahine* [grandmother] left me a *kukui* nut *lei* when she died. The nuts were strung on black, silk threads from an old dress of hers. I suppose that at some time I was told the significance of the *lei*, but didn't pay any attention. Then it was put away for safekeeping and forgotten. But, now that I knew the importance of *kukui*, I realized that this would be my gift to the king, my friend.

The next morning I took the *lei* from my dresser drawer, carefully wrapped it in fine cotton, placed it in a *ti* leaf *pū'olo*, or package, and, like Lovey, gave it to one of the palace servants to give to the king. Because of the importance of *kukui* and the Hawaiian love of *lei*, I hoped he would be pleased.

I was right. He sent me a thank you letter, again on 'Iolani Palace stationery, saying my gift showed that I understood the importance of *kukui*, and therefore it was a special *ho'okupu*. He wrote that he would always think of me when he wore it. He included a printed invitation to his birthday ball, knowing I would like the keepsake to remind me of that special day and all the events that went along with it. At the top of the thick white card was a gold engraving of the king's crown with the red cap, resting on a gold cushion. A wide gold band, with a narrow red outline, went around the inside edges of the card. My full name, Māhealani Kau'i Kanahele, was written in fancy calligraphy by one of the chamberlain's secretaries.

When the time comes, I will give the two thank you letters, the invitation, and these written memories of a by-gone era to my own children. And the *lei kukui*.

The *lei* has gone full circle. Sadly, King Kalākaua died four years later, just after his 54th birthday. Several months later Queen Dowager Kapi'olani

invited me to "Pualeilani," her home in Waikīkī, located in a shady, cool coconut grove not far from ʻĀinahau, the Cleghorn home. The queen moved there after the king's death, leaving the palace to the new monarch, Queen Liliʻuokalani.

I crossed the verandah and was escorted by a female friend of Queen Kapiʻolani into a large, cool room. After I curtsied to her she invited me to sit with her on a plush circular sofa that came from ʻIolani Palace. The room was filled with a mixture of Hawaiian, European, Oriental and American furniture, including a piano, and smaller items such as family photos and many plants. I recognized one of the huge bronze Chinese vases and the Ipu Makani O Laʻamaomao, the wind container, also from the palace. Papa told me that when the queen removed her personal belongings from the palace she was allowed to purchase certain items that were owned by the government.

Queen Kapiʻolani handed me the *lei kukui*, wrapped in *kapa*. She rarely used the English language, so spoke to me in Hawaiian, saying "I want you to have this, Māhealani, as a reminder of the king's fondness for you. He received many gifts for his 50th birthday, gifts he liked and appreciated, but they were mostly bought gifts. Your gift of a family *lei* was a gift of the heart. This meant a great deal to him, and he mentioned your generosity every time he wore it.

I now return it to you and your family."
Pretending I hadn't seen the tears form in her
eyes as she talked of the king I thanked her,
curtsied again, and left.

I have never worn the *lei*, and it has always held
a place of honor wherever I have lived. I smile
when I look at it, sometimes also shedding a few
tears for those royal days of long ago.

My *keiki* and *moʻopuna*, my children and
grandchildren, will be living in a world quite
different from mine, but these memories and
mementos will help them to learn and understand
a rich and elegant part of their *waiwai hoʻoilina o
Hawaiʻi*, their Hawaiian heritage.

ENDNOTES

[1] 'Iolani means royal hawk. The high flight of the hawk symbolized Hawaiian *ali'i*.

[2] The men following the *kāhili* bearers were the Hon. William C. Parke, marshal of the kingdom; the Hon. John M. Kapena, minister of finance; the Rev. Canon Alexander Mackintosh of St. Andrew's Cathedral and chaplain of the royal household; the Hon. Geoffrey Rhodes, president of the legislature, and the Hon. Francis A. Judd, chief justice.

[3] In ancient times *pūlo'ulo'u* were made of a stick or spear topped with a *kapa*-covered ball. It was a symbol of *kapu* which was carried before a chief and signified his sacred presence. They were also used as stationary markers to show the boundaries of a chief's enclosure. The entrance to the enclosure was sacred, no one was permitted to linger there. Upon approaching a *pūlo'ulo'u* an invited visitor would be required to show signs of humility, such as laying flat on the ground face down, or removing his *kapa* cloak, wrapping it in a *pū'olo*, or bundle, and covering it with grass. At times it was necessary to approach crawling, so as not to let a shadow fall on the chief.

[4] Queen Kapiʻolani's ladies-in-waiting were Mrs. Charles H. Judd, Mrs. Curtis P. Iaukea, Mrs. Colburn, Miss Lucy Pohaialiʻi, Mrs. Alfred N. Tripp and Mrs. Maria King. In attendance on Her Royal Highness Princess Liliʻuokalani were Mrs. Charles B. Wilson and Miss Sophia Sheldon. Her Royal Highness Princess Likelike was attended by the Misses Clara (Clarissa) and Lizzie (Elizabeth) Coney.

[5] Prince David Piʻikoi Kawānanakoa was the eldest son of Princess Kinoike Kekaulike and High Chief David Piʻikoi. He was born in 1868 and died in 1908. He married Abigail Campbell, daughter of Abigail Maʻipinepine and James Campbell. They had three children: Abigail Kapiʻolani, David Kalākaua and Lydia Liliʻuokalani Kawānanakoa.

[6] This is often erroneously referred to as "Cry out, O Isles, with joy!," which is actually the first line of the third stanza. The anthem was composed by Mr. Wray Taylor, organist at St. Andrew's Cathedral.

[7] It is thought by many today that "*i ka pono*" should be translated to mean "when things are properly ordered" or "when things are as they should be" or "in rightness." Understanding the difference in meaning requires an understanding of the situation at the time the statement was

made. This occurred after an incident in 1843 in which the British consul laid claim to Hawaiian kingdom property, a claim not recognized by King Kamehameha III. The incident and speech can be found in many Hawai'i history books. For an explanation of the translation of the motto see MAN, GODS, AND NATURE by M. K. Dudley.

[8] This is the second statue. The first statue was cast in Paris, France, in 1878, and shipped to Hawai'i from Bremen, Germany. The ship it was on hit a reef, caught fire and sank during a storm off Port Stanley in the Falkland Islands in 1880. It eventually turned up (in poor condition) in Port Stanley, was purchased by an English sea captain who brought it to Honolulu in 1882 and sold it to King Kalākaua. In the meantime a replica was made in Paris and arrived in Honolulu just two weeks before King Kalākaua's coronation ceremony. The replica was used in the ceremony and is the one in Honolulu. The original was sent to 'Āinakea in Kohala, on the island of Hawai'i, in 1883. In 1912 it was moved to the grounds of the courthouse at Kapa'au in Kohala.

[9] "Lovey" was the real name of a real cat owned by King Kalākaua.

[10] Hale 'Ākala, the king's bungalow, was a two-

story wood bungalow, used as a private retreat, on the Richards and Hotel Streets corner of 'Iolani Palace. It was torn down in 1919 because of extensive termite and wood rot damage.

[11] Most of the palace furniture was made by the Davenport Company in Boston, Massachusetts, which later made furniture for the White House.

[12] The Kamehameha Cloak is at Bishop Museum, where it has been since 1893. E. H. Bryan, Jr., an international authority on the natural history of Pacific islands and affiliated with Bishop Museum for over 60 years (at one time Curator of Collections), calculated the total number of feathers in the cloak to be about 450,000. With a bird generally furnishing only six or seven appropriate feathers, more than 80,000 birds would have been required to make the cloak.

[13] This *pūloʻuloʻu* was presented to King Kalākaua by Captain Alfred N. Tripp. He took the ivory stalk from a narwhal whale he killed off Cape Serdze in the Arctic Ocean. A friend of King Kalākaua, he was appointed "Special Commissioner for Central and Western Polynesia," a job intended to promote good relations between the Hawaiian government and the Gilbert Islands.

[14] Siam is now Thailand, Prussia is now Germany,

and Austria\Hungary are now two separate countries.

[15] The Ipu Makani O La'amaomao is on display in Hawaiian Hall of the Bishop Museum. There is a book on the subject, <u>The Wind Gourd of La'amaomao</u>, by Esther Mookini and Sarah Nākoa.

BACKGROUNDS OF REAL CHARACTERS

* The marshal of the kingdom was a high-ranking law enforcement officer. He was, among other things, in charge of keeping the public peace and carrying out executive mandates of the king and executive departments of government.

* The chamberlain was overseer of the royal household, in this case 'Iolani Palace.

KALĀKAUA, David La'amea Kamanakapuu Mahinulani Naloiaehuokalani Lumialani.

> Reigned 1874 to 1891 as King Kalākaua. Son of High Chief Kahanu Kapa'akea and High Chiefess Analea Keohokalole. Born in Honolulu November 16, 1836. Married Julia Kapi'olani Nāmākēhā December 19, 1863. Died in San Francisco January 20, 1891. No children.

KAPI'OLANI, Julia Nāpelakapuokaka'e.

> Reigned as Queen Kapi'olani as wife of King Kalākaua. Daughter of High Chiefess Kino'iki (daughter of King Kaumuali'i of Kaua'i) and High Chief Kūhiō. Born in Hilo, Hawai'i, December 31, 1834. Married Chief Benet Nāmākēhā March 8,

1852. Widowed December 1859. Married High Chief David La'amea Kalākaua December 19, 1863. Widowed January 20, 1891. Died in Honolulu June 24, 1899. No children.

LILI'UOKALANI, born Lili'u Loloku Walania Wewehi Kamaka'eha, generally called Lili'u or Lydia, her baptismal name.

> Reigned 1891 to 1893 as Queen Lili'uokalani, the name given to her by her brother, King Kalākaua, when he named her heir apparent and Princess in 1877. Daughter of High Chief Kahanu Kapa'akea and High Chiefess Analea Keohokalole. Born in Honolulu September 2, 1838. Married John Owen Dominis September 16, 1862. Widowed August 27, 1891. Died November 11, 1917. No children.

IAUKEA, Curtis Pi'ehu.

> Served five monarchs, holding nearly every government position under King Kamehameha V through the Territory of Hawai'i, retiring from public office in

1919. Chamberlain to King Kalākaua from 1886 until the king's death in 1891. Born in Kohala, Hawai'i, December 13, 1855. Son of Lapaha (daughter of Kalanipō, a Chief of the "Ī" and "Mahi" clans of the Kohala and Hāmākua districts of Hawai'i) and John W. Iaukea of Hāmākua. Married Charlotte Kahālo'ipua Hanks of Honolulu April 7, 1877. Died in Honolulu May 5, 1940. Two children.

IAUKEA, Charlotte Hanks.

Born in Honolulu September 9, 1856. Daughter of Akini Tai Hoon and Frederick Leslie Hanks. (Her father's antecedents were the same as those from whom Nancy Hanks, mother of President Abraham Lincoln, was descended.) Married Curtis Pi'ehu Iaukea April 7, 1877. Died November 17, 1939. Two children.

JUDD, Charles Hastings.

Held numerous government positions under three rulers, from King Kamehameha V to King Kalākaua. Chamberlain to King Kalākaua until his resignation in 1886, when he was succeeded by

Col. Curtis Pi'ehu Iaukea. Born in
Honolulu September 8, 1835. Son of
Dr. Gerrit Parmele Judd and Laura
Fish Judd. Married Emily Catherine
Cutts in Honolulu, 1859. Died in Kualoa,
O'ahu, April 4, 1890. Four children.